Judith Harries

50

fantastic **ideas**
inspired by **famous artists**

FEATHERSTONE

FEATHERSTONE

Bloomsbury Publishing Plc

50 Bedford Square, London, WC1B 3DP, UK

BLOOMSBURY, FEATHERSTONE and the Feather logo are trademarks of Bloomsbury Publishing Plc

First published in Great Britain 2018 by Bloomsbury Publishing Plc

Text copyright © Judith Harries, 2019

Photographs © Shutterstock, 2019

A catalogue record for this book is available from the British Library

ISBN: PB: 978-1-4729-5684-2; ePDF: 978-1-4729-5685-9

2 4 6 8 10 9 7 5 3 1

Series design: Lynda Murray

Printed and bound in India by Replika Press Pvt. Ltd.

To find out more about our authors and books visit www.bloomsbury.com and sign up for our newsletters

Contents

Introduction

The most significant word in the title of this book is 'inspired' as that is the intention of this collection of ideas – to show children evidence of art around them and inspire them to join in creative activities at whatever level they are at. Children should be inspired by what they see, hear, feel and experience in your setting. This used to be referred to as 'awe and wonder', an expression I still like to use, and was generally used in the context of being amazed by the natural world. I like to think it can also be applied to the world of art.

All EYFS settings need to provide opportunities for children to explore expressive art and design activities and the current trend for continuous provision requires that resources for this are made freely available for children to select from during each session.

In this child-initiated environment, it is important that practitioners don't get too hung up or fixated on 'end products', as there is definitely no 'right' and 'wrong' in artistic endeavour. The learning is in the 'doing'. It is not my intention

that children should be expected or even coerced into imitating or producing exact copies of the artworks featured in this book. They can instead learn from the methods, techniques or intention of each artist. Don't forget to be creative yourself. Try out some of the activities, before, during or after you have shared them with the children.

> *Every child is an artist, the problem is staying an artist when you grow up.*
> **Picasso**

Let the children's interests initiate an activity and then you can try to extend their learning by introducing a relevant artist or style of painting. For example, if a child says 'I want to paint a picture of me', show them some examples of portraits by Kahlo or Picasso, and if another child is really keen on cutting, explore the work of Matisse or Apfelbaum. Other artworks will suggest themselves during planned topic work – explore Turner's paintings of the sea during a holiday theme or Delaunay's work on circles when looking at shapes.

The activities and artists in this book are subdivided into helpful sections – drawings, portraits, still life, landscapes, abstract, shapes and patterns around the world, sculpture, collage, pop and street art, and contemporary. Many of the activities start with an exploration stage allowing children to experiment with the resources. Children often need lots of investigative time especially if materials and techniques are new. The idea of inspiring children through famous artist's work is to take their ideas to the next step. Most activities work best with small groups so adult support is more easily available if requested. The introduction to the artwork can be presented to the whole group via an interactive whiteboard or computer.

Useful resources

Most of the resources required are easily accessible and will be already available in your setting. Clearly, some of the activities require forward planning, as do many art activities, but it is still possible to organise them quite spontaneously if your resource area is kept well stocked. Here are some ideas to start you off:

- **Paper** – different sizes of white and coloured paper; tissue paper; lining paper; cardboard; packaging

- **Drawing** – pencils, 3B–HB; pencil crayons; wax crayons; oil pastels; felt pens; charcoal; chalks; sketch pads; clip boards; whiteboards and pens

- **Painting** – powder paints; ready mix paints; watercolours; spray paint; different-sized brushes; rollers; sponges; palettes; paint pots; easel

- **Collage** – newspapers; magazines; sheet music; boxes; wrapping paper; string; wool; glitter; beads; sequins; buttons; ribbons; pompoms; fabric; lolly sticks; art straws; bubble wrap; dry pasta

- **Sculpture/modelling** – clay; play dough; salt and flour dough; clay tools; cutters; rolling pins; junk boxes and tubes; wood; modroc; wire; pipe cleaners; plastic bottles; lids; balloons

- **General** – scissors; glue; sticky tape; guillotine; sand; water; washing-up liquid.

Using this book

It is a good idea to read through each activity before you start in case you want to change the order or just focus on one part. Anything is possible! The pages are all organised in the same way under the following headings:

What you need lists the items needed for each activity. This always starts with a suggestion for the famous artwork to be located online. A quick image search will usually find multiple versions of the picture and some will allow you to print as well. Access to Wi-Fi and the means to display pictures on an interactive whiteboard or computer is an essential requirement.

Top tips give a brief word of advice or helpful tip that could make all the difference to the experience of the activity for you and your children.

What to do provides step-by-step instructions on how to present the idea. There are often alternative routes to take as well if children are particularly keen on one aspect of the activity. Pick and choose the activity depending on the interests of children in your setting, the resources and time available.

Taking it forward does exactly that – takes the activity to another level, often by introducing a new artist or suggesting further activities related to the original idea.

What's in it for the children? lists some of the benefits to the children and describes how the activity will help children develop across the Early Learning Goals.

Health and safety is a helpful warning or suggestion included if appropriate.

Meet the artist includes names, dates, and interesting facts about each artist alongside a summary of their contribution to art and the occasional enlightening quote.

Stick figures (Klee)

Try some scratch art

What you need:

- Access online to images of 'Portrait of an Equilibrist', 'Fish Magic' or 'The Goldfish' by Klee
- Shallow tray
- Dry sand
- Sticks
- Paper
- Wax crayons or oil pastels
- Black paint
- Washing-up liquid
- Blunt pencils or clay tools

Top tip

Use small pieces of thick paper as they are quicker to fill and will cope with being coloured, painted and scratched!

What's in it for the children?

Everybody can have a go at this simple representation of human or animal figures.

Taking it forward

- Let children experiment with drawing stick people in lots of different ways using pencils, pens and chalks. Look at images of stick people such as cave paintings; Chaz Hutton, who draws his figures on sticky notes; and Stik, a graffiti artist.

- Watch some stick figure animations on YouTube™ to give the children some more ideas for their pictures.

- Look at the work of L.S. Lowry, who was famous for his paintings of 'matchstick men, cats and dogs'.

What to do:

1. Start by sharing Klee's quote (see below) and let children draw in a tray of dry sand using their index finger or a small stick.

2. Show the children images of 'Portrait of an Equilibrist'. Can they see the two ways this painting can be seen – as a stick man and a face? Explain that 'equilibrist' is another word for an acrobat.

3. Look at Klee's images of fish in 'Fish Magic' or 'The Goldfish'. How does he make the colours appear so vivid?

4. Help children to prepare some 'scratch' paper by making stripes of brightly coloured wax crayons or oil pastels.

5. Add a squirt of washing-up liquid to some black paint and paint over the colours.

6. Let children use blunt pencils or clay tools to scratch their own pictures and portraits.

Paul Klee (1879–1940) loved drawing and one of his most famous quotes is that 'a drawing is simply a line going for a walk'. He is well known for his simple stick figures and using very bright colours.

Just a line (Picasso)

Simple line drawings of animals

What you need:

- Access online to images of some of Picasso's line drawings
- Whiteboards and pens or paper and pencils
- Charcoal
- Paper
- Chalk
- Black sugar paper
- String
- Glue

Top tip ⭐

Let children practise their drawings on whiteboards, wiping away any pictures they are not pleased with. Take photos of all of the successes!

What's in it for the children?

Children will experience the importance of practising and persevering until they are satisfied with their work.

Taking it forward

- Make a collection of famous cartoons or illustrations of animals for children to compare, trace and copy. Try 'Bambi', 'Tigger', 'Peppa Pig', 'Hello Kitty' and 'The Gruffalo'!

- Compare with the elaborate style of Albrecht Dürer and his woodcut pictures 'Rhinoceros' and the watercolour 'Young Hare'.

- Go to www.differantly.com and look at more single line drawings by Differantly (aka DFT).

What to do:

1. Show the children some images of Picasso's line drawings of animals such as 'Dog', 'Penguin', 'Camel', 'Flamingo', 'Sparrow' and 'Mouse'. How many of them can the children name?

2. Point out to the children that many of Picasso's drawings are done with one single line.

3. Provide children with whiteboards and pens, or pencil and paper, so they can practise drawing simple shapes using a single line. Let them see what they can draw without taking their pencil off the page.

4. Try drawing animals with charcoal on white paper or white chalk on black sugar paper.

5. Challenge children to use a length of string and glue to make the shape of an animal stuck down on black sugar paper.

6. Can they devise their own signature like Picasso to identify their work?

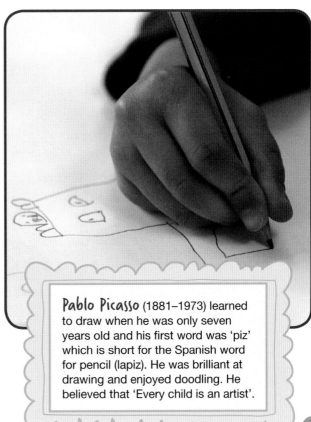

Pablo Picasso (1881–1973) learned to draw when he was only seven years old and his first word was 'piz' which is short for the Spanish word for pencil (lapiz). He was brilliant at drawing and enjoyed doodling. He believed that 'Every child is an artist'.

A famous lady (Da Vinci)
Painting portraits to order

What you need:

- Access online to images of 'Mona Lisa' by Da Vinci
- Magazines
- Paints and brushes
- Palette
- Easel
- Cardboard
- Pasta
- Gold paint

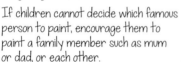

Top tip ⭐

If children cannot decide which famous person to paint, encourage them to paint a family member such as mum or dad, or each other.

What's in it for the children?

Painting a portrait requires children to look closely at what they are trying to represent. Encourage careful observation and use of realistic colours if possible.

Taking it forward

- Children can take it in turns to sit as models for each other to paint. How does it feel to sit still for more than one minute?

- Look at portraits of women by other famous artists and compare them: 'Girl with a Pearl Earring' by Vermeer and 'Portrait of Madame X' by John Singer Sargent.

What to do:

1. Explain to children that painting portraits of people is a very old art form that many 'Old Masters' have tried.

2. Show the children images of the 'Mona Lisa' painting and talk about who they think she was. What do the children think she was thinking about while she was being painted?

3. Explain to the children that they are going to choose a famous person and paint their portrait. Let them look through magazines to choose their subject.

4. Talk about choosing a head and shoulders portrait or a full-length picture.

5. Look at different skin tones with the children and encourage them to experiment with different colours in their palettes.

6. Invite children to paint their portraits on an easel like a professional artist.

7. Make the children's paintings look suitably grand by adding a frame made from cardboard and pasta, sprayed with gold paint.

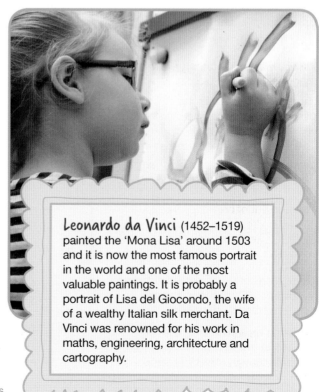

Leonardo da Vinci (1452–1519) painted the 'Mona Lisa' around 1503 and it is now the most famous portrait in the world and one of the most valuable paintings. It is probably a portrait of Lisa del Giocondo, the wife of a wealthy Italian silk merchant. Da Vinci was renowned for his work in maths, engineering, architecture and cartography.

Fruity portraits (Arcimboldo)
Creative fruit and vegetables

What you need:

- Access online to images of 'Vertumnus', 'The Summer' or 'Fruit Basket' by Arcimboldo
- Fresh fruit and vegetables
- Large serving plate
- Pencils and crayons
- Paints and brushes
- Paper
- Magazines
- Scissors
- Glue

Top tip ⭐

Supermarket magazines are a good source of pictures of fruit and vegetables for children to use.

What's in it for the children?

Children will enjoy creating pictures using an unusual medium such as fruit and vegetables, and it should provide lots of opportunities for conversation.

Taking it forward

- Compare these paintings with the artworks of pop artist Jason Mecier, who creates portraits out of food such as 'Big Bird' made out of breakfast cereal. Let the children have a go at using cereal, lentils or beans to create a portrait.

- Arcimboldo's 'Reversible Head with Basket of Fruit' and 'The Vegetable Gardener' pictures look like 'still life' paintings when turned upside down. Show the children how this works. Look at other examples of optical illusions.

What to do:

1. Show the children pictures of Arcimboldo's fruit and vegetable portraits. How many different types of fruit and vegetables can they spot?

2. Let children experiment with their own choice of fruit and vegetables to create a 'fruity portrait'. Which fruit would work well for a mouth? How could they create hair?

3. Let the children take turns to arrange their choices on a large plate. Take a photo of each face.

4. Invite them to transfer their ideas to paper. Draw or paint a picture of their 'fruity face', using the photographs you took as reference.

5. Alternatively, let them find pictures of different fruit and vegetables in magazines and cut out, arrange and stick down their favourite version.

6. Wash the fruit and vegetables after you have finished with them and let the children make some salads to share at snack time.

> **Guiseppe Arcimboldo** (1527–1593) is well known for painting fruity portraits including 'Vertumnus' (1590/91), which is a picture of his boss, the Holy Roman Emperor. Now, many of his pictures are used by advertisers to sell healthy food!

Painting selfies (Kahlo)

Look in the mirror and what do you see?

What you need:

- Access online to images of some of Kahlo's many self-portraits
- Mirrors
- Photographs of children
- Paper
- Pencils and crayons
- Paints and brushes
- Palette
- Painting easel

Top tip

Children can also use photographs of themselves to help with their self-portraits.

What to do:

1. What do children understand by the term 'self-portrait'? Are they the same as 'selfies'? How do they think artists paint pictures of themselves?

2. Show the children images of Kahlo's self-portraits. Point out that she often concentrated on painting her own face in close-up.

3. Let children use mirrors and their photographs to look at their faces close-up. Talk about the different features they can see.

4. Ask children to draw a simple sketch of their face using pencils and crayons. What colour will they choose for their eyes, hair or skin?

5. Help children to mix colours in a palette to create different skin tones.

6. Invite children to paint their self-portraits using the easel like an artist and referring to their pencil pictures.

7. Display the self-portraits alongside the pencil sketches and photographs.

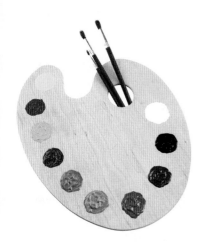

What's in it for the children?

Children will enjoy using paints to represent their own ideas about themselves and to compare their features, faces and feelings with others.

Taking it forward

- Many of Kahlo's self-portraits include spider monkeys, parrots or dogs. Ask children to choose a soft toy or pet animal to include in their painting.

- Look at some more examples of self-portraits by other famous artists such as Rembrandt, Van Gogh or Amrita Sher-Gil. Many of Van Gogh's self-portraits include him wearing a hat or smoking a pipe! Ask children to choose one prop to add to their next picture such as a hat, toy or piece of jewellery.

- Arrange an exhibition of the children's paintings so parents and carers can see them. Display them with labels turned to the wall to see if parents can recognise their children. Sell them to raise funds!

Frida Kahlo (1907–1954) was a Mexican artist who painted 55 portraits of herself, including several with animals. She had a serious accident in her teens and was forced to recover in a body brace so she used a special easel so she could paint in bed. 'I paint self-portraits because I am so often alone, because I am the person I know best.'

Life-size moving pictures (Himid)

Posing and painting people on the move

What you need:

- Access online to paintings of people by Himid such as 'Naming the Money' and 'Between the Two my Heart is Balanced'
- Large piece of cardboard
- Chalks
- Scissors or a craft knife
- Paints and brushes

Top tip ★

Let children take turns to draw around each other with chalk as if at a crime scene! Invite them to create different body shapes on the floor.

What's in it for the children?

Children will enjoy showing good control and coordination in large and small movements by turning them into still poses.

Taking it forward

- Show the children examples of some flip-book animation on YouTube™.
- Staple together some mini-books for them to create their own flip-books by drawing stick men or other pictures.
- Look at the work of Edgar Degas, a French artist who painted many pictures of dancers on the move.

✚ Health & Safety

Take care using scissors and always supervise handling craft knives.

What to do:

1. Show the children images of people painted by Himid. 'Naming the Money' is made up of colourful cut out figures.

2. Go outside and play a game of 'musical statues'. Point out some good statue poses for children to observe.

3. Talk about different dancing and sports that the children are involved with. Are there any dancers or gymnasts who could demonstrate their skills?

4. Ask all the children to find a space in the room. Let them strike some different poses that they might make while running, jumping, hopping, dancing, kicking a ball, and so on. Take photographs.

5. Choose a child to lie on the floor on top of a large piece of cardboard and create an active body shape such as running or kicking. Draw round the shape in chalk and cut it out using scissors or a craft knife.

6. Try painting the body outline with bright colours to create a cut out portrait.

7. Repeat with a different pose and stand up the moving portraits around the room.

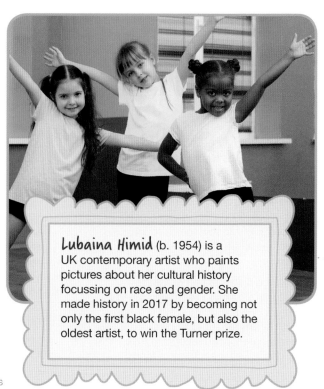

Lubaina Himid (b. 1954) is a UK contemporary artist who paints pictures about her cultural history focussing on race and gender. She made history in 2017 by becoming not only the first black female, but also the oldest artist, to win the Turner prize.

Both sides now (Picasso)

Create a two-faced portrait

What you need:

- Access online to images of Picasso's various paintings of 'Dora Maar', 'The Weeping Woman' and others
- Paper
- Paints and brushes
- Black marker pen

Top tip ⭐

Spend some time with the children observing the differences between a profile and full–face view in pictures.

What's in it for the children?

This activity helps children to see things from different angles and to develop a sensitivity to each other's needs and feelings by closely observing facial expressions.

Taking it forward

- Go to www.picassohead.com/create.html and let children create their own Mr Picasso Head-style picture. Simply click and drag faces, eyes, noses, lips and hair to create a fun image.
- Try a collage-style portrait using cut-out faces and features from magazines. Cut a picture into lots of small pieces and then stick them down in a random order to create a cubist portrait.
- Look at the Repligator at www.ransen.com, which uses an effect or filter to turn a photograph into a cubist painting like Picasso or Georges Braque!

What to do:

1. Look at a selection of Picasso's paintings of women that famously show the profile and the full face in one picture.

2. Can the children see what the painter has done? Talk about where the different features of the face are positioned.

3. Ask children to practise drawing faces from different angles using the paper, paints and brushes. How many eyes can they see in a profile picture? Can they see all of the mouth?

4. Challenge them to paint a portrait in the style of Picasso. Encourage them to use brightly coloured paints and bold shapes in the portrait.

5. Provide less confident children with a framework for the Picasso portrait: give them a face template that has been cut in half down the centre.

6. Add an outline to the pictures with a black marker pen.

7. Look at 'Girl before a Mirror' and talk about the different angles the children can see. Use two children to create a real-life representation of this. Can they mirror each other's actions?

Pablo Picasso (1881–1973) was one of the founders of the cubist movement, which specialised in showing objects or figures from different angles and was one of the first abstract art styles.

Mystery portraits (Magritte)

Making the everyday look different

What you need:

- Access online to images of 'The Son of Man' or 'Man in a Bowler Hat' by Magritte
- Magazines
- Scissors
- Paints and brushes
- Paper
- Glue

Top tip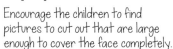

Encourage the children to find pictures to cut out that are large enough to cover the face completely.

What's in it for the children?

This activity challenges the children to use their imaginations and have fun mixing and matching random objects. They can use knowledge of shapes to describe the objects they choose.

Taking it forward

- Look at 'The Portrait' – a painting that combines still life and portraiture. Make a list of the items in the picture. Let children use a collection of items to create a new picture. It must contain at least one facial feature!

- Show children a photograph of the artist with his hat on upside down. Let the children take photos of each other wearing their hats upside down.

Health & Safety

Take care using scissors. Provide left-handed scissors where required.

What to do:

1. Show the children the image of 'The Son of Man' and/or 'Man in a Bowler Hat'. What do the children notice about the paintings?

2. Explain that they are going to choose a random object to add to a portrait. Let them look through magazines to find a suitable picture to cut out. It could be a piece of fruit, a round biscuit or an animal.

3. Ask the children to paint a portrait or self-portrait. You could use a photocopy of a previous painting.

4. Help them to stick the chosen picture onto their painting, directly over the face. Enlarge the picture if it is not big enough to cover the face.

5. Alternatively, find a copy of Magritte's painting online. Let children use software such as RM Colour Magic to draw a new object, or use the stamp icon, over the top of the apple. What other changes could they make?

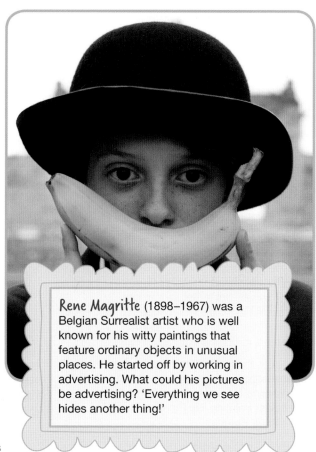

Rene Magritte (1898–1967) was a Belgian Surrealist artist who is well known for his witty paintings that feature ordinary objects in unusual places. He started off by working in advertising. What could his pictures be advertising? 'Everything we see hides another thing!'

Photo shopping (Leibovitz)

Take some photo portraits

What you need:

- Access online to some of Leibovitz's photographic portraits
- Digital camera
- Printer

Top tip

Make sure that children know to always ask permission before taking a photo of somebody.

What's in it for the children?

They will have an opportunity to handle cameras and use simple technology as part of this activity.

Taking it forward

- Ask children to look through magazines and newspapers to find examples of good photographic portraits.

- Check out some other famous portrait photographers such as Steve McCurry ('Afghan Girl'), Lisa Kristine and Shirin Neshat.

- Look at the work of photo-realist artist Bradley Hart who creates portraits by injecting bubble wrap with paint! The pictures appear pixelated as though on a screen. Let the children experiment with painting patterns onto bubble wrap by painting individual bubbles with small brushes.

✚ Health & Safety

Make sure you check that parental permission has been obtained if displaying photos of children in your setting or online.

What to do:

1. Look at photos taken by Leibovitz of a variety of celebrities including the Queen, John Lennon and many different actors.

2. Choose two contrasting photos for the children to compare. How is the person standing or sitting? Are they posing or does it look natural? Are they holding anything?

3. Let children practise taking photos of each other using a digital camera. Can they tell each other how to sit, stand or pose for the portrait? Do they want anything else in the photo?

4. Ask children to think about the setting for their photographs. Try taking photographs inside and outside.

5. Show them how to delete photos that they are not pleased with. Ask them to choose one favourite picture to print for a display.

Annie Leibovitz (b.1949) is an American portrait photographer. She has worked for many magazines including 'Vanity Fair' and 'Rolling Stone'. She recently took some exclusive photos of the cast involved in the Star Wars 'The Last Jedi'.

Still fruity (Cézanne)

Painting things that keep still

What you need:

- Access online to images of 'Still Life with Apples', 'Apples and Oranges' or 'Four Apples' by Cézanne
- A selection of fruit, e.g. apples, oranges, lemons, cherries, bananas
- A tray
- Tablecloths or fabric
- Paper and pencils
- Paint, brushes and palettes
- Other items or containers to paint, e.g. bottles, baskets, bowls, jugs, pots, vases
- Shallow paint trays

What to do:

1. Look at images of still life paintings by Cézanne. Introduce the term still life. Can the children work out why it is called this?

2. Start by asking the children to choose some fruit to draw and/or paint. Ask them to work together to arrange it on a tray.

3. How many apples or oranges have they chosen? Will they look best placed in a straight line or balanced on top of each other? Are they all the same colour or the same size?

4. When they are happy with the arrangement, the children can draw the fruit and then paint them.

5. Challenge children to try a more complicated arrangement, using more fruit and some containers. Does adding vases, bottles or bowls make their pictures more interesting?

6. Finally, share the fresh fruit together at snack time.

Top tip ★

Encourage the children to spend time arranging the fruit and other objects until they are happy with the effect, before they start to draw or paint.

✚ Health & Safety

If the fruit is to be eaten after it has been used as a 'model', make sure it is washed thoroughly.

What's in it for the children?

These varied activities will involve lots of different sensory experiences for the children. Working together to create an arrangement will encourage them to take pride in their artwork.

Taking it forward

- Let children choose some different objects to arrange and paint such as vegetables, other food items, flowers, pottery, cloth, and so on.

- Look at some other still life artists who painted fruit such as Caravaggio or Monet.

- Try some other fruity art techniques. Cut some of the fruit in half and try printing a fruity pattern using a shallow tray of paint.

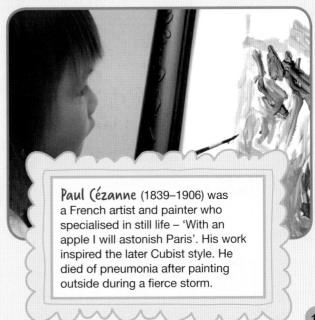

Paul Cézanne (1839–1906) was a French artist and painter who specialised in still life – 'With an apple I will astonish Paris'. His work inspired the later Cubist style. He died of pneumonia after painting outside during a fierce storm.

Take three things (Valadon)

Create a picture using three contrasting objects

What you need:

- Access online to images of 'Still Life with Fruit', 'Still life with Bowl of Fruit, Flowers and Onions', 'Still Life with Herring' and 'The Violin Case' by Valadon

- Lots of different items for children to select from, e.g. fruit, vegetables, flowers, fish, candles, lights, shells, toys, musical instruments

- Pencils and pens

- Paints and brushes

- Paper

- Camera

What's in it for the children?

Children can use their imagination to look at and use objects and materials in different and original ways.

Taking it forward

- Compare these paintings with other still life artists such as Morandi, Braque and Picasso.

- Look at Picasso's construction 'Still Life' (1914). This goes beyond painting and uses 'found objects' to create a 3D still life artwork.

- Let the children find three different objects, arrange them, photograph them and show them as 'found still life' creations.

✚ Health & Safety

Take care handling items, especially found objects, that may have potential for splinters or scratches.

What to do:

1. Look at some images of Valadon's still life paintings. What do the children notice about them? Can they always tell what the pictures are?

2. Ask children to choose three contrasting objects to arrange and rearrange.

3. Challenge them to look at the shapes and colours of the different objects they have selected. What happens if they move one of the objects round to show it at a different angle?

4. When they are pleased with the layout they have made, invite them to draw or paint a still life picture.

5. Take a photograph of the objects to display alongside the finished artwork.

Top tip

Encourage children to spend time arranging their three things before they decide on the best layout for their artwork.

Suzanne Valadon (1865–1938) was a French artists' model who became an artist in her own right after an accident on the trapeze ended her career in the circus. She had always loved drawing as a child and when money was short she used charcoal and scraps of paper.

Giant flowers (O'Keeffe)

Painting big, bold, beautiful flowers

What you need:

- Access online to images of 'Red Poppy' or 'The White Trumpet Flower' by O'Keeffe
- Real flowers to observe
- Sketching materials, e.g. pencils and paper
- Magnifying glasses
- Paints and brushes
- Palettes
- Giant sheets of paper

What's in it for the children?

Children will be actively involved in comparing size as they look at real and painted flowers.

Taking it forward

- Look at some other examples of famous paintings of flowers or plants such as 'Sunflowers' by Van Gogh, 'Water Lilies' by Monet and 'Ten-Foot Flowers' by Warhol.

- Try using some cut sponges or potatoes to print repeated flower shapes in the style of Warhol's painting.

- Look at 'Puppy' by Jeff Koons, for another way to use flowers in art! This is a living sculpture where the flowers are still growing. Let the children create their own collage of a flowery pet by sticking dried flowers and moss onto a template of a cat or dog.

What to do:

1. Look at some of O'Keeffe's paintings. Why do the children think she painted such giant pictures of flowers?

2. Go outside and encourage children to sketch any flowers they can see. Can they keep their drawings life-sized?

3. Provide a selection of real flowers for the children to smell, handle (gently), draw and paint. Let them use magnifying glasses to look close up at the flowers.

4. Ask children to choose a colour of paint such as red, pink or purple and then create lots of different shades of the same colour by gradually adding white paint.

6. Challenge the children to fill the whole of a large sheet of paper with their flower painting. They can draw the shape first if that helps.

6. Let the children choose a different subject for another giant picture such as a plant, toy, pet, and so on.

Top tip ★

Take a photo of any flowers the children are painting in case the blooms don't survive the creative experience.

Georgia O'Keeffe (1887–1986) was an American artist who is best known for her paintings of enlarged flowers. She felt that flowers were too small and wanted people to see how beautiful they were.

Stretching the imagination (Dali)

Enjoy making real things look unreal

What you need:

- Access online to images of 'Clock Explosion' or 'The Melting Watch' by Dali
- Analogue clocks and watches
- Soft play dough
- Cardboard
- Markers
- Circle templates
- Old magazines or newspapers
- Scissors
- Glue

What to do:

1. Show children images of 'Clock Explosion' or 'The Melting Watch' by Dali. Talk about how the clock has been stretched because the artist liked to challenge the way people look at things.

2. Provide some clocks and watches for children to handle and look at closely.

3. Let them make some flat clock faces, circles and ovals out of soft play dough.

4. What happens when the clocks are placed on the edge of the table? With a little help, they will stretch!

5. Ask children to draw circles onto the cardboard using different-sized circle templates. Can they cut them out and draw numbers on them to create clock faces?

6. Create a clock explosion collage using the cardboard clock faces, pictures of clocks and watches cut out of magazines. Add cut-outs of different-sized numbers which use a variety of fonts.

Top tip ★

Use a rolling pin to stretch the play dough clocks into a more 'stretchy' shape.

What's in it for the children?

Children can arrange materials in original ways to represent their own ideas and use their imaginations.

Taking it forward

- Look at some more examples of Dali's artworks such as 'The Elephants' and 'Lobster Telephone'. How do the children react to the strange images he portrays? Can they think of some other odd combinations to put together?

- Show the children a photo of the artist. Does he look as they expected?

✚ Health & Safety

Take care using scissors. Provide left-handed scissors where required.

Salvador Dali (1904–1989) was a Spanish artist who was highly imaginative and rather eccentric. He was a 'surrealist', which means 'beyond reality'. He enjoyed putting unexpected things together in one picture, such as the lobster and the telephone!

The great wave (Hokusai)
Water paintings

What you need:

- Access online to images of 'The Great Wave off Kanagawa' by Hokusai
- Photographs of the sea, waves and other watery landscapes
- Shallow trays with dry sand
- Felt pens
- Paper
- Combs
- Paints
- Old boxes and scissors or wood

What's in it for the children?

Children will develop control and coordination in large and small movements. They will gain an understanding of the purpose of backgrounds and foregrounds in a picture.

Taking it forward

- Try some other watery styles such as magic painting. Use white candles or white wax crayons to draw wave patterns on paper. Cover with a thin wash of blue paint and see how the picture emerges like magic.

What to do:

1. Show the children images of this wood print by Hokusai. What else can they spot in the picture? They might notice: three boats with rowers clinging to their oars, Mount Fuji, the artist's signature.

2. Look at the shapes of the waves. Search for photographs of big waves online and compare them to the wood print.

3. Make some big wave shapes with your arms and ask children to copy. Encourage big, bold movements.

4. Let them practise drawing waves in dry sand using their fingers.

5. Try drawing wave patterns using felt pens on paper. Use lots of different colours and thicknesses of pens.

6. Model using combs to apply paint to paper to make wave patterns using blue and white paint. Give children an opportunity to try this method.

7. Cut old boxes into A4 size pieces or use pieces of wood if available. Let children cover them with white paint.

8. When the white background is dry, use combs to paint blue waves on top in the foreground.

Katsushika Hokusai (1760–1849) was born in Edo (now Tokyo) in Japan. He is best known as a printmaker and his series of woodcuts, 'Thirty-six Views of Mount Fuji', includes this painting of the Great Wave.

In the wash (Turner)

Paint the sea as you see it

What you need:

- Access online to images of 'Norham Castle, Sunrise', 'Seascape with a Sailing Boat and a Ship' and 'Snow Storm' by Turner
- Photographs of the sea
- Thick paper
- Watercolour paints and brushes
- Water
- Tissue or paper towels

Top tip

Take care when working with wet paper as it becomes very fragile!

What to do:

1. Show the children some images of Turner's seascape paintings and talk about what they can see in the pictures.

2. Explain that Turner used watercolours to paint an impression of what he saw.

3. Look at a variety of photographs of the sea in all its different moods – calm, rough, big waves, stormy, night and day, showing boats being tossed about, people surfing, and so on.

4. Let the children experiment with watercolour paints.

5. Ask them to brush clean water all over a piece of paper. Then add thin streaks of different watery colours – blue, yellow, grey, green – to try and create the effect of painting the sea. The wet background allows the colours to run and blend and create a blurry impressionistic effect.

6. Show children how to use tissue or paper towels to blot their painting to remove paint and create the effects of waves and clouds on their pictures.

7. When the pictures are dry, let the children add a tiny outline of a sailing boat, person, tree or island onto the picture using a small paintbrush or black pen.

What's in it for the children?

Children can enjoy painting an impression of what they see and experimenting with colour, design and form.

Taking it forward

- Compare Turner's paintings of the sea with 'The Great Wave' by Hokusai (p.21).

- Try the reverse water effect. Allow children to paint a picture and then spray water onto it so that the colours run and dribble as though it has been raining.

- Let children (dressed appropriately) paint outside on a rainy day!

- Show children the work of artist Marc Allante at http://www.marcallante.com/album/silhouttes.html. He specialises in using dripping paint to create a rainy day effect.

William Turner (1775–1851) was an English painter known particularly for his watercolour landscapes and paintings of the sea. He took his sketchbooks with him every day so that he could paint what he saw. One famous story says he tied himself to the ship's mast so he could experience a storm first-hand.

Starry, starry night *(Van Gogh)*
Painting in the dark

What you need:

- Access online to images of 'The Starry Night' by Van Gogh
- Paints and brushes
- Cotton buds
- Paper
- Cardboard
- Aluminium foil
- Dark blue paper
- Black paper
- Scissors
- Glue

What to do:

1. Look at images of 'The Starry Night' and talk about what the children can see in the painting. How do they know that it is night-time? Compare with photographs of landscape and city scenes taken at night.

2. Point out the spirals and swirls that Van Gogh used to create the effect of the moon and stars shining in the sky.

3. Let children practise painting these shapes using cotton buds, small brushes and/or fingers onto different types of paper or even cardboard covered in aluminium foil.

4. Now encourage them to paint the moon and stars in white and yellow paint onto dark blue paper for the night sky.

5. Help children to cut shapes out of black paper for the foreground. Try outlines of buildings, trees and other shapes and stick them onto the front of their painting with glue.

Top tip ⭐

Encourage children to practise drawing spiral shapes in the air with their fingers before trying to paint them.

What's in it for the children?

Children can explore features of their environment at night and use their imaginations to express their ideas.

Taking it forward

- Read *Katie and the Starry Night* by James Mayhew.

- Look at the painting 'Starlight Night' by Georgia O'Keeffe and compare how she created the effect of stars to Van Gogh's technique.

- Try some other painting effects for stars, such as using toothbrushes to flick paint onto black paper, dabbing cotton buds to remove paint and adding sequins and sticky stars.

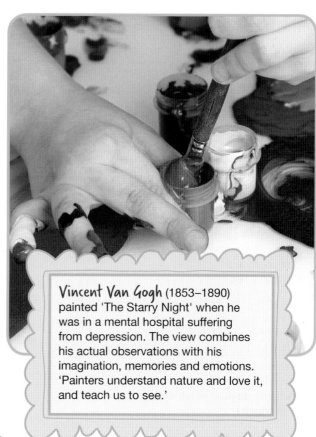

Vincent Van Gogh (1853–1890) painted 'The Starry Night' when he was in a mental hospital suffering from depression. The view combines his actual observations with his imagination, memories and emotions. 'Painters understand nature and love it, and teach us to see.'

View from an open window (Matisse)

A favourite view

What you need:

- Access online to images of 'The Open Window, Collioure' by Matisse
- Photographs or postcards of different views and landscapes
- Camera
- Paint and brushes
- Magazines
- Scissors
- Corrugated cardboard

What to do:

1. Ask children to look out of the window and talk about what they can see. Do they like the view?

2. Show them images of Matisse's painting. What could the painter see? Which colours did he choose to use?

3. Look at a variety of photos or postcards showing views. Take photos of views from the windows at your setting. Ask children to bring in photos from home of views out of windows.

4. Invite children to paint pictures of their favourite view. Alternatively, children can select a favourite postcard or picture from a magazine to use as their view.

5. Construct window or picture frames out of corrugated cardboard to frame children's favourite views.

Top tip

If children don't have access to a window with a special view, let them use their imaginations. What would they like to see out of the window?

Health & Safety

Remind children to only look out of a closed window, especially if it is upstairs!

What's in it for the children?

Children are encouraged to look at features of their own environment and think about how environments might vary from one to another.

Taking it forward

- Share *Window*, by Jeannie Baker, with the children. In this wordless picture book, the scene changes through the window as the boy grows up, shown through a series of mixed-media collages. Let children use collage materials to create their own view from the window.

- Read *Matisse, King of Colour* by Laurence Anholt and find out more about Matisse's love of colour.

- Compare with the work of Gabriele Münter, who painted stylised landscapes in unusual colours.

Henri Matisse (1869–1954) was a French artist known for 'wild' use of colour in his paintings. He first started to paint when his mother bought him some paints after he had been ill. 'From the moment I held the box of colours in my hand, I knew this was my life.'

Compositions (Kandinsky)

Painting with lines, shapes and colours

What you need:

- Access online to images of 'Composition VIII' and 'Composition X' by Kandinsky
- Templates of some Kandinsky shapes
- Black felt pen
- Sticky paper
- Scissors
- Different coloured paper
- Paints and brushes
- Ruler

Top tip ⭐

Make the shape templates out of stiff cardboard and not too small, so children can handle them easily.

What's in it for the children?

Children can learn to distinguish between geometric shapes and irregular shapes. They can learn to handle tools such as pens, scissors and rulers to good effect.

Taking it forward

- Kandinsky may have suffered from 'synaesthesia', and associated particular colours and marks with specific sounds. Invite the children to choose a piece of music to play while they paint.

- Read *The Noisy Paint Box: The Colors and Sounds of Kandinsky's Abstract Art* by Barb Rosenstock.

➕ **Health & Safety**

Take care using scissors. Provide left-handed scissors where required.

What to do:

1. Show children images of 'Composition VIII' and 'Composition X' by Kandinsky.

2. Compare what they can see in the pictures. Explain that 'abstract art' means that the artist is not trying to 'represent' any specific things.

3. Provide templates of some of the irregular shapes Kandinsky used. Children can draw round these on sticky paper and cut them out to add textures to their own paintings.

4. Ask them to choose some coloured paper (not black) for the background of their picture.

5. Can they paint lines, patterns and shapes onto their 'composition' and then stick on some irregular shapes?

6. Leave the painting to dry. Encourage the children to finish by drawing some straight lines, and adding hatching and cross-hatching using a pen and ruler on top of the paint.

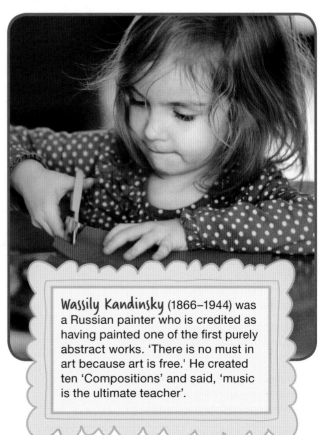

Wassily Kandinsky (1866–1944) was a Russian painter who is credited as having painted one of the first purely abstract works. 'There is no must in art because art is free.' He created ten 'Compositions' and said, 'music is the ultimate teacher'.

The colour orange (Miró)
A journey into one colour

What you need:

- Access online to images of 'The Orange Hypnotiser' by Miró
- Orange cardboard or sugar paper
- Black paint
- A variety of paintbrushes, combs, sponges, forks, cotton buds, toothbrushes
- Black felt pens, different thicknesses

Top tip

Demonstrate some of the techniques children could use with the comb, fork, sponge and other tools.

What's in it for the children?

Handling different tools to apply the paint will increase children's fine motor skills. Colour mixing is fun and will lead to the discovery of lots of different shades.

Taking it forward

- Talk about the colour orange. How many different orange things can the children think of? Show the children how to make orange by mixing yellow and red together.

- Look at works by Mark Rothko – who also liked to use just a few colours in a painting – such as 'Orange, Red, Yellow'.

- Miró also painted a series of paintings inspired by the colour blue. Choose a different colour background such as purple. Explore how to make purple using red and blue, then paint using one colour such as white or yellow.

What to do:

1. Show the children an image of 'The Orange Hypnotiser' by Miró.

2. Talk about what they notice. Miró only uses one colour with lots of different ways of applying the black paint.

3. Make a list of any shapes the children see. They will notice different things and there is no right or wrong answer. Encourage them to use their imaginations.

4. Will they include an 'eye' shape in their painting? Let them choose a different shape to add such as a face, an arrow or a star.

5. Provide each child with a piece of orange card or paper, a pot or tray of black paint and a selection of tools.

6. Let them experiment with different tools to create black images on the orange background.

7. Add finishing touches using black felt pens or crayons.

Joan Miró (1893–1983) was a Spanish painter and sculptor who also made ceramics. He went to his first drawing class aged seven and at the age of 82 he started painting with his fingers. He was friends with Pablo Picasso and visited his studio many times.

Spray it again (Pollock)

Paint, paint everywhere

What you need:

- Access online to images of 'Convergence', 'Lavender Mist' or 'No. 5' by Pollock
- Large sheets of black paper
- Small squeezy bottles (or pipettes, syringes, basters)
- Different colours of runny paint
- Toothbrushes
- Spray paints
- Water pistols
- Sticks, trowels and plastic knives

What to do:

1. Look at images of paintings by Pollock that use dripping paint. Watch a video online of him at work.

2. Explain to children that they are going to work together in a group to create a giant Pollock-style painting.

3. Start with a giant piece of black paper (or several pieces joined together) and stick it to the floor.

4. Give each child a small squeezy bottle of paint or a pipette, syringe or baster. Let them drip, pour, squeeze, shoot, fling, splatter and scrape their paint onto the picture.

5. Model how to use a toothbrush to splatter paint, preferably in the right direction, so that paint can reach the middle of the paper.

6. Use spray cans or water pistols to add to the effect. Encourage the children to scrape the applied paint with sticks, trowels and plastic knives.

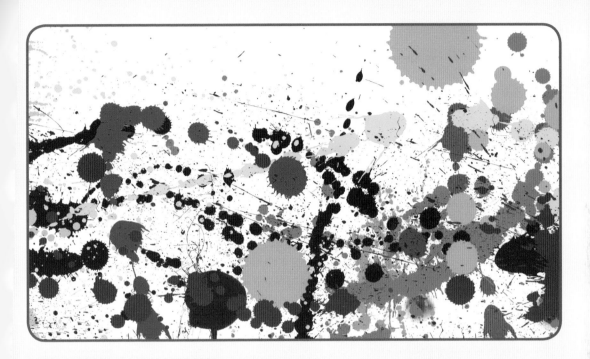

What's in it for the children?

Children work as part of a group, cooperating with each other and understanding the need to follow rules.

Taking it forward

- Read *Jackson Pollock (Getting to Know the World's Greatest Artists)* by Mike Venezia.

- Let children have a go at creating individual paintings in this style.

Jackson Pollock (1912–1956) was an American artist famous for using the 'drip' method to cover huge canvases that he placed on the floor of his studio. 'The painting has a life of its own. I try to let it come through.'

Aboriginal dots

Using dots to create pictures and patterns

What you need:

- Access online to images of Aboriginal art
- Templates in various shapes, e.g. fish, bird, lizard
- Black paper
- Cotton buds, sticks and straws
- Red, brown, orange, yellow, white and black paint
- Clay
- Clay tools

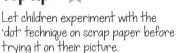

Top tip ⭐

Let children experiment with the 'dot' technique on scrap paper before trying it on their picture.

What's in it for the children?

Children can use small tools delicately and effectively to create striking symbolic pictures from another culture and tradition.

Taking it forward

- Look at the work of Queenie McKenzie, an Australian artist, who painted pictures of her native country and used dots to add outlines.
- Look at the work of George Seurat, pointillist artist, who painted with points or 'dots' to create pictures such as 'A Sunday Afternoon on the Island of La Grande Jatte'.
- Bradley Hart creates pixelated pictures by injecting bubble wrap with liquid paint. Let children paint bubble wrap with different colours and then create some press prints.

What to do:

1. Search online for images of Aboriginal art to show the children. Make a list of the natural earth colours used, e.g. red, brown, orange, yellow and black.
2. Talk about the pictures they can see, such as hands, fish, lizards, flowers, and so on.
3. Provide children with templates of a fish, bird or lizard to draw round at the centre of their picture. Alternatively, they can draw round their hand on black paper.
4. Use a cotton bud or stick and one colour to make dots or spots all around the outline of the picture.
5. Build up the picture using further layers of dots and spots in natural colours.
6. Use some of the techniques to create a clay tile. Provide children with a flat square tile of clay and show children how to make small indents or dots into the clay using clay tools.

Aboriginal art, the art of indigenous Australians, uses symbols such as animals, natural items and patterns to communicate about their lives. It is one of the oldest art forms around today.

Islamic geometry
Using repeated patterns and symmetry

What you need:

- Access to online images of Islamic geometric art
- Spirograph Jr™
- Pens
- Coloured paper
- Scissors
- Symmetrical pattern templates
- Circles of coloured paper
- Thick cardboard
- Sticky tape or glue

Top tip

Cut the dome arch out of cardboard packaging using a utility knife. Children can watch you do this.

What's in it for the children?

Lots of practise using tools such as Spirograph Jr™ and scissors will help develop children's fine motor skills.

Taking it forward

- Look at Islamic calligraphy art using Arabic letters and compare with the illuminated letters used in Celtic art. Make copies of children's initial letters for them to draw or colour in.

- Make some individual repeated patterns using cut out stars or flower shapes in different types of paper.

Health & Safety

Show children how to handle scissors and other tools safely.

What to do:

1. Search online for images of Islamic art and talk about the colours, repeated patterns and symmetry in the designs. Look at examples of Islamic architecture too.

2. Show children how to use the Spirograph Jr™ tool to create symmetrical patterns on coloured paper. Cut out some of the circles.

3. Find symmetrical patterns online and print them out for children to colour in. Cut out the finished artwork.

4. Try some symmetrical cut out shapes. Start with a circle of coloured paper – fold it in half, and then in half again. Help children to cut out holes along the folds. Open it out and ask children to decorate with repeated patterns.

5. Cut out a large arch or dome shape from thick cardboard.

6. Arrange the different circles in a variety of ways to create patterns. When the children are pleased with the combination, stick the circles onto the cardboard arch.

7. Hang the arch up over a doorway to create a display.

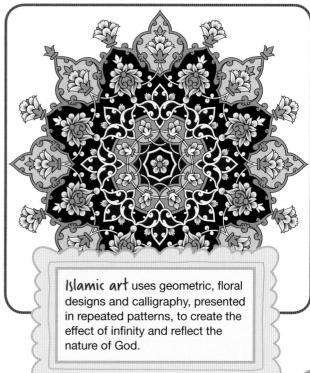

Islamic art uses geometric, floral designs and calligraphy, presented in repeated patterns, to create the effect of infinity and reflect the nature of God.

Rangoli rings

Creating colourful decorations and patterns

What you need:

- Access to online images of Rangoli patterns
- Outside area
- Hula hoop
- Coloured chalks
- Coloured sand
- Rice
- Seeds
- Lentils
- Flowers
- Cardboard
- Glue, in a squeezy bottle
- Powder paint

What to do:

1. Show the children online images of Rangoli patterns. Talk about their use in decorating homes during Diwali or to celebrate birthdays and weddings.

2. Go outside on a dry day and choose a suitable site for the Rangoli ring.

3. Start by drawing round a large hula hoop using chalk. Then let children take turns to draw more concentric circles inside the ring. Fill in the rings with different coloured chalks using colouring, hatching and blocking techniques.

4. Layer different materials on top of the chalks. Try coloured sand, rice, seeds, lentils, dried flowers, and so on.

5. Let children create individual Rangoli patterns on small squares of cardboard.

6. Draw round a circle template and then squeeze glue on to the circle outline. Sprinkle coloured sand and powder paint onto concentric rings inside the circle.

Top tip ⭐

If the weather is wet, don't despair – chalk circles on the playground floor will look even brighter.

What's in it for the children?

Children will become aware of the similarities and differences between themselves and others through enjoying the art of another culture.

Taking it forward

- Search online and download Rangoli designs for children to colour in.

- Look at another ancient Indian art form called Warli. This uses white paint on rich earth-coloured backgrounds and is noted for the use of stick figures made out of triangles and circles. Let children have a go at drawing and painting these figures.

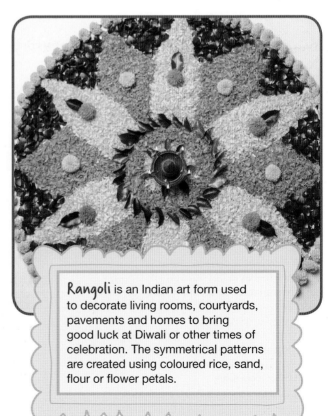

Rangoli is an Indian art form used to decorate living rooms, courtyards, pavements and homes to bring good luck at Diwali or other times of celebration. The symmetrical patterns are created using coloured rice, sand, flour or flower petals.

Mexican weaving

Create a Mexican God's Eye

What you need:

- Access to online images of Mexican God's Eye
- Lollipop sticks or twigs
- Glue or twine
- Colourful wool
- Beads or feathers

Top tip ★

Try using variegated wool – the colour changes are all done for you.

What's in it for the children?

Children develop sensitivity and understanding of other cultures through exploring and creating traditional art.

Taking it forward

- The indigenous people of Mexico also made pictures or 'yarn art' by gluing wool onto wooden boards to create shapes inspired by nature. Popular images are snakes and birds. Help children to draw a snake and/or bird and then use different coloured wool to create a collage picture.

- Try some Mexican tin art. Cover a paper plate with aluminium foil and let children use tools to create lines and patterns around the rim, leaving the centre free like a mirror. Add paint in bright colours or use marker pens.

✚ Health & Safety

Show children how to handle scissors and other tools safely.

What to do:

1. Show children images of Mexican God's Eyes online. These decorative shields were made so that the gods could keep an eye on people and protect them from harm.

2. Glue or tie two lollipop sticks or twigs together into a cross shape.

3. Fasten a length of wool onto the centre of the cross. Show children how to wrap the wool over and around one stick, and then move on a diagonal to the next stick and repeat.

4. Carry on until the 'eye' or block of colour is the required size and then change colour by attaching a new length of wool.

5. Let children decorate their weaving with feathers at the end of each stick and thread beads onto the wool as they weave.

This traditional **Mexican craft** originates from the Huichol, the indigenous people of Mexico. The four points of the 'eye' were said to represent the four elements – fire, earth, air and water – and the centre was believed to provide protection from the gods.

Mosaic castles (Klee)

Using shapes to create a castle in the sky

What you need:

- Access online to images of 'Castle and Sun' by Klee
- Coloured building bricks
- Camera
- Coloured chalks
- Sticky paper shapes
- Dark blue paper
- Sponge blocks or potato stamps
- Shallow trays of paint

Top tip ⭐

Use small pieces of sponge pre-cut into squares or rectangles to create the mosaic effect.

What's in it for the children?

Building with bricks and then art materials will enable children to handle tools effectively and combine this with an imaginative use of shapes and patterns.

Taking it forward

- Look at 'Madame Kupka among Verticals' by Frank Kupka. Can they spot her face peering out from the shapes? Let children use a camera to take selfies, print them out, mount on paper and paint stripes of colour around the face to create a pattern frame.

- Beg, buy or borrow a set of PicassoTiles® and let children use these magnetic plastic tiles to construct imaginative buildings inspired by Paul Klee.

What to do:

1. Look at Klee's painting 'Castle and Sun'. How many different colours and shapes can the children see?

2. Start by building 3D sculptures of castles using coloured building bricks. Take photographs of the finished models.

3. Let children go outside with coloured chalks and create some pavement art using blocks of colours. Can they work together to draw a castle on the floor?

4. Provide children with lots of pre-cut stickers of geometric shapes. Include lots of different-sized rectangles, squares and triangles but only one circle.

5. Ask them to build a mosaic castle, tower or other fine building by sticking the shapes onto a piece of dark blue paper.

6. Try making printed mosaic pictures of buildings using sponge blocks or potato halves dipped into shallow trays of paint.

Paul Klee (1879–1940) was a Swiss artist well known for his use of vibrant blocks of colour. He said 'To paint well is simply this: to put the right colour in the right place.'

Concentric circles (Delaunay)

Painting a circle inside a circle, inside a circle...

What you need:

- Access online to images of 'Prismes électriques' or 'Propeller' by Delaunay
- Coloured chalks
- Hula hoops
- Paint and brushes
- Lots of different-sized circle templates
- Large piece of cardboard
- Glue

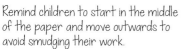

Top tip ⭐

Remind children to start in the middle of the paper and move outwards to avoid smudging their work.

What's in it for the children?

Children can compare quantities and size, recognise patterns and explore shapes, using mathematical language, as they get creative collaboratively.

Taking it forward

- Try producing a collage version of the concentric circles. Provide lots of circle templates, coloured paper, scissors and glue for children to create collage circles.

- Look at 'Colour Study, Squares with Concentric Circles' and 'Several Circles' by Kandinsky. Children can add their circle paintings to squares cut out of coloured paper. Let children use cups and corks to print different-sized outlines and solid circles onto black paper.

- Show children 'Rhythm' by Robert Delaunay, Sonia Delaunay's husband, who also had a 'thing' about concentric circles.

What to do:

1. Show children the paintings online and point out the geometric shapes.

2. Let children experiment by drawing different coloured circles inside each other using chalk. Try on paper or outside on the pavement. Encourage them to draw really large shapes using hula hoops.

3. Explain that you are going to work together to create a giant painting using these shapes.

4. Count how many different rings or circles are used to create Delaunay's painting. Decide if children want to stick to this number or try a new arrangement.

5. Show children how to paint the concentric circles onto smaller pieces of paper, starting with the smallest circle in the centre first and moving out. Some children may choose to use circle templates, others may paint freehand.

6. Display alongside other artwork inspired by Delaunay and Kandinsky (see **Taking it forward**).

Sonia Delaunay (1885–1979) was a Ukrainian artist who lived and worked in Paris with her husband Robert. Her work was known for its use of geometric shapes, in particular circles. She also worked in textiles and had an interior design and fashion boutique called Casa Sonia.

Primary shapes (Mondrian)

Arranging red, blue and yellow shapes and lines

What you need:

- Access online to images of 'Composition II in Red, Blue and Yellow' by Mondrian
- Coloured Duplo™
- White paper
- Squared paper
- Coloured and black felt pens
- Ruler
- Red, blue and yellow paper
- Scissors
- Glue
- Primary colour paints
- Black paint

What to do:

1. Show children images of Mondrian's paintings using red, blue and yellow shapes. Identify the shapes and colours.

2. Let children use Duplo™ to create 3D versions of the paintings. Place a choice of five or six bricks onto white paper and then draw straight lines, up and down, using black felt pen and a ruler.

3. Provide squared paper and let children draw a series of black lines, criss-crossing and intersecting each other. Colour in some of the shapes that are created using red, yellow and blue felt pens.

4. Invite children to cut squares and rectangles out of primary-coloured paper and stick down onto paper. Intersect the shapes again with straight black lines.

5. Challenge the children to paint versions of the Duplo™ and paper pictures using primary colours. Add black lines at the end using a thin paintbrush and a ruler.

6. Alternatively, start by ruling black lines with a felt pen onto the paper. Then paint in blocks of colour where they intersect.

7. Create a display using all the different artworks inspired by Mondrian's art.

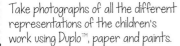

Top tip ⭐

Take photographs of all the different representations of the children's work using Duplo™, paper and paints.

✚ Health & Safety

Take care using scissors. Provide left-handed scissors where required.

What's in it for the children?

Children can choose different materials and ways to represent their ideas involving primary colours, simple shapes and straight lines.

Taking it forward

- Show children images of Mondrian-inspired artwork that uses Lego™ bricks for inspiration.

- Look at Mondrian's penultimate painting 'Broadway Boogie Woogie'. Talk about how this is different from the earlier works. Mondrian was inspired by the blinking lights and traffic moving around the city, as well as jazz music. Encourage children to use rulers and yellow, red and blue felt pens to create their own cityscape.

- Let children explore the 'Mondrimat' game at http://www.stephen.com/mondrimat, an online game that lets them experiment with colours and shapes. Model on the whiteboard first to show children how to use the game.

Piet Mondrian (1872–1944) was a Dutch painter who specialised in geometric abstract works using primary colours, red, yellow and blue. His work formed the 'De Stijl' or 'The Style' movement in art.

50 fantastic ideas inspired by famous artists

Optical illusions (Riley)

Making moving black and white patterns

What you need:

- Access online to images of 'Movement in Squares' and 'Fall' by Riley
- Black and white paper
- Black and white paint
- Pieces of thick cardboard – 12cm by 5cm
- Scissors
- Glue
- Black and white ribbons

Top tip ⭐

Let children lead this activity and create their own interpretations of Op art using the materials provided.

What's in it for the children?

Children can explore new ways of looking at shapes and patterns and present their ideas in original designs.

Taking it forward

- Look at 'Zebras' by Victor Vasarely, the 'grandfather' of Op art. Can the children see the animals in the picture? Use black and white paint to create zebra paintings.

- Paint an Op art pot. Let children paint a small flowerpot white all over and then add a black stripe, zigzag or spotty Op art design.

What to do:

1. Show children some of Riley's 'Op art' paintings. How does looking at the paintings make the children feel? Do the patterns seem to move as they look at them?

2. Start with a simple painting. Ask children to cover their white paper with thin black paint or black paper with white paint.

3. Help them to make a 'line-making tool' by cutting triangles out of the edge of a thick piece of cardboard to create a comb effect.

4. Use the cardboard tools to draw parallel lines in the paint. They can be straight or wavy.

5. Cut lots of small black and white squares and rectangles out of paper. Can children stick them into a chessboard pattern all over their paper?

6. Look at Riley's 'Arrest' series. Try sticking white and black ribbons onto paper in parallel lines. Make some of the ribbons wavy and some straight.

Bridget Riley (b. 1931) is an English artist who paints in the Op art style, creating optical illusions and movement as you look at the pictures. 'I work with nature, although in completely new terms'.

Spot the dots (Kusama)
Fabric painting and printing

What you need:

- Access online to images of some of Kusama's paintings and installations such as 'Dots Obsession'
- Cotton buds
- Paint
- Paper
- Sponges cut into circles
- Coloured paper
- Fabric paints and pens
- Plain squares of cotton
- Old white t-shirts

What's in it for the children?

Painting and printing onto fabric requires a lot of physical coordination and fine motor dexterity.

Taking it forward

- Look at Kusama's sculpture 'Pumpkin'. Try some new painted pumpkin designs for Halloween!

- Show the children Damien Hirst's spot paintings. Let them print their own colourful spot pictures using corks or sponge balls.

- Try some hole punch art. Punch holes all the way around a small circle of coloured card. Empty the hole punch and stick the dots in the middle of the card.

✚ **Health & Safety**

Show children how to use the hole-punch safely so that no fingers are hurt in the process.

What to do:

1. Look at images of Yayoi Kusama and her work online. She is obsessed with polka dots, both in her work and on her clothes.

2. Start by making miniature polka dot pictures using cotton buds, paint and small pieces of paper.

3. Let children use sponges to try some dot printing with colourful paint onto coloured paper.

4. Experiment with fabric paint on scrap pieces of fabric before moving onto the t-shirts.

5. Ask parents to bring in an old white t-shirt from home and let the children use the fabric paint to cover it with polka dots.

6. Invite parents and friends to come to a fashion show where children can show off their dotty t-shirts and artwork.

Yayoi Kusama (b. 1929) is a contemporary artist from Japan who has recently achieved fame through her obsession with dots. She is usually seen wearing clothes patterned with dots and her paintings and installations feature dots and spots everywhere. There is a museum celebrating her work in Tokyo.

Walking man (Giacometti)

Create some stick figure sculptures

What you need:

- Access online to images of 'Man Pointing', 'Walking Man' or 'The Chariot' by Giacometti
- Jumbo pipe cleaners
- Garden wire
- Aluminium foil

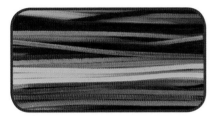

Top tip ⭐

Allow children plenty of opportunities to experiment with the pipe cleaners and garden wire so that they can manipulate them more effectively.

What's in it for the children?

Children will safely use and explore a variety of materials and tools and experiment with the form and shape of human and animal figures.

Taking it forward

- Show children images of 'The Dog' by Giacometti and 'The Spider' by Louise Bourgeois. Can they create their own animal sculptures using wire, pipe cleaners, aluminium foil and clay?

- Look at Giacometti's sculpture 'The Nose'. Relate this to the Pinocchio story. Let children create their own heads with long noses using malleable clay or play dough. Who can make the longest nose?

What to do:

1. Show children pictures of Giacometti's magnificent sculptures, often of human figures. What do the children notice about these figures? Point out the very thin, stretched limbs.

2. Let children handle pipe cleaners and/or garden wire to create their own stick figures.

3. Allow lots of time for children to experiment with the wire and use their own ideas to create sculptures of shapes, figures and patterns.

4. Move on to showing children how to bend the wire and make a circle for the head.

5. Attach more pipe cleaners to make the body and limbs of the figure. Will the sculpture be walking or pointing?

6. Wrap strips of aluminium foil around the figure to create the effect of metal.

7. Display the figures together in a group on a flat surface, or add some wheels and put the figure in its own chariot.

Alberto Giacometti (1901–1966) was a Swiss sculptor and painter. He started off by creating small figures – seven centimeters was the size of the biggest ones – and then he moved onto making the tall, slender, elongated figures for which he is now famous.

Making art move ((alder)

Make a moving mobile

What you need:

- Access online to images of 'Antennae with Red and Blue Dots', 'Mobile' and 'Hanging Spider' by Calder
- Metal coat hangers
- Garden wire
- Pipe cleaners
- Pieces of plastic, stiff fabric, coloured card, etc.
- Shape templates
- Scissors
- Hole punch
- String

What to do:

1. Ask children who they think invented mobiles (the hanging kind)? Show children images of Calder's mobiles.

2. Talk about the different materials he used to create the sculptures. Describe the shapes – triangles, circles, plectrums, teardrops, squares, and so on.

3. Make a collection of different materials that children can choose to use.

4. Let them use different-sized shape templates to cut shapes out of a selection of materials. They will need about seven or eight shapes to create a mobile.

5. Show them how to make holes in the plastic or fabric using a hole punch.

6. Help the children tie different lengths of string onto each shape and then attach to a metal coat hanger or a cross made out of garden wire or pipe cleaners.

Top tip ★

Let children practise making holes in paper before progressing onto more tricky materials.

What's in it for the children?

Children can identify shapes and sizes and use mathematical language as they construct their mobiles.

Taking it forward

- Look at 'Fish', 'Flying Fish', 'Goldfish Bowl' and 'Aquarium', all works by Calder inspired by fish. Let children experiment with wire, pipe cleaners and shapes to create their own wire sculptures.

- Listen to John Cage's 'Music for "Works of Calder"' online. It sounds like the mobiles are bumping into each other as they hang in the air.

Health & Safety

Show children how to use the hole punch safely.

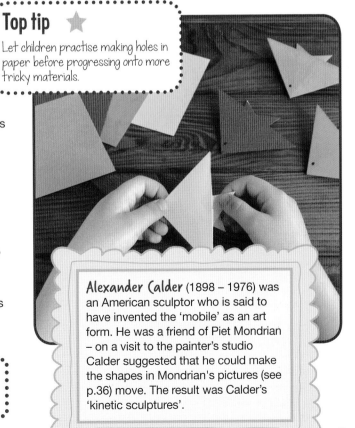

Alexander Calder (1898 – 1976) was an American sculptor who is said to have invented the 'mobile' as an art form. He was a friend of Piet Mondrian – on a visit to the painter's studio Calder suggested that he could make the shapes in Mondrian's pictures (see p.36) move. The result was Calder's 'kinetic sculptures'.

Walk-thru art (Moore)

Taking junk modelling to a new level

What you need:

- Access online to images of 'Large Arch', 'The Arch', 'Figure in a Shelter' and other large-scale sculptures by Moore

- An outside area

- Junk, e.g. lots of large cardboard boxes, buckets, tubes

What to do:

1. Look at images of Moore's 'The Arch' sculptures. He wanted people to be able to walk through his artworks!

2. Explain to the children that they are going to build some large-scale models using junk materials.

3. Go outside and sort junk materials by size, shape and purpose. Talk about columns, walls and arches.

4. Let children work with a partner or in a small group to build a tower or wall using boxes and other junk.

5. Supervise and advise where it is needed. Will this bucket make a better base for the column or pillar? How could we put this box on top of here? Let's try turning it the other way round.

6. Try joining two columns together with a plank to make the arch for the children to walk through.

✚ Health & Safety

Supervise construction activities at all times so children are not put at risk.

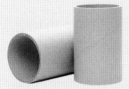

What's in it for the children?

Children can work together to construct giant models, safely negotiating each other and the space available.

Taking it forward

- Another artist who liked a building challenge was Constantin Brancusi. His 'Endless Column' was built in 1938 as a memorial to soldiers who died in WWI. How high can the children build a tower with their junk materials? Which group can build the highest structure?

- Show children images of the supersize pop art sculptures made by Claes Oldenburg such as 'Clothespin', 'Spoonbridge and Cherry' and 'Dropped Cone', which features a giant ice cream cone!

- Look at 'Sky Cathedral' by Louise Nevelson. Let children create a 3D sculpture stuck onto a piece of cardboard and then paint it one colour.

- Compare these sculptures with the work of Rachel Whiteread, who makes sculptures from casts. Use clay and plaster of Paris to create casts of children's hands, feet and other 'impressionable' objects!

Henry Moore (1898–1986) was one of the most famous British artists. He liked to make large outdoor sculptures and many of his artworks can be seen on display in parks and cities. 'As a young sculptor I saw Stonehenge and ever since I've wanted to do work that could be walked through and around.'

Holes and halves (Hepworth)

Creating shapes and making holes

What you need:

- Access online to images of 'Single Form', 'Two Forms (Divided Circle)', 'Corinthos' and 'Summer Dance' by Hepworth
- Clay or play dough
- Clay or play dough tools, e.g. rolling pin
- Ruler
- Shape cutters

Top tip ⭐

Let children have plenty of time to handle and manipulate the clay before trying to create shapes.

What's in it for the children?

Children can explore using clay with their hands and then handling tools to create different shaped holes.

Taking it forward

- Compare with 'Magic Mask' by Elizabeth Catlett, a sculpture that is loosely based on an African mask. Let the children make faces or clay masks with holes for the eyes, nose and mouth.
- Look at the work of Henry Moore, another famous British sculptor who created large abstract-shaped artworks. He created a sculpture called 'Mother and Child', as did Hepworth a couple of years before him. Look also at 'Recumbent Figure' and 'Animal Head'. Let the children use play dough or clay to create solid shapes and figures.

What to do:

1. Show the children some images of Hepworth's bold sculptures. What do they notice that the artworks have in common?

2. Explain that they are going to use clay or dough to create their own shapes with holes.

3. Ask them to choose a shape to start with – a rectangle, oval, square or triangle. Can they make the shape freehand so it's not too 'perfect'? Press it or use a rolling pin to flatten the shape.

4. Use a ruler to draw a line down the centre of the shape. Cut it and divide into two halves.

5. Use a shape cutter to make a hole in each half. Stand up the two shapes so they can be seen as a whole again.

6. The wonderful thing about clay is that the shapes can then be combined and worked with again and again.

Barbara Hepworth (1903–1975) was an English sculptor and one of the only women artists of her generation to be recognised internationally. Her studio and home in St Ives in Cornwall is now a museum.

Giant creatures (Saint-Phalle)

Work together to make giant colourful creations

What you need:

- Access online to images of 'Fish', 'Nana on a Dolphin' and 'Serpent Tree' by Saint-Phalle
- Balloons
- Newspaper
- Glue
- Paints and brushes
- Cardboard
- Garden wire
- Modroc
- String
- Boxes

Top tip ⭐

Make sure the children have aprons to wear as this could be a very messy activity.

What's in it for the children?

Children will work cooperatively in small groups to produce larger scale artworks. They need to listen to each other's opinions and ideas.

Taking it forward

- Experiment with other ways to create and sculpt different shapes. Try filling rubber gloves with plaster of Paris to make model hands in the style of 'The Cathedral' by Rodin or 'Welcoming Hands' by Louise Bourgeois.

- Look at pictures of buildings and the 'Parc Güell' designed by the Catalan architect Gaudi, who inspired Niki de Saint-Phalle to create her own 'The Tarot Garden'.

What to do:

1. Show children images of sculptures by Saint-Phalle online. Try to show them in situ so that children can get some idea of how big they are.

2. Explain that they are going to create their own sculpture inspired by her fish or snake (serpent) shapes.

3. Partially inflate balloons, round or long shaped, and show children how to cover them with torn strips of newspaper dipped in glue to create layers of papier-mâché. Leave each layer to dry.

4. Paint the fishes and snakes with brightly coloured stripes and add eyes. Attach matching stripy cardboard tail fins to the tied end of the balloon for the fishes.

5. Make some larger scale shapes and creatures using garden wire, newspaper and modroc for the children to paint in small groups. Emphasise the use of strong colours and rounded shapes.

6. Display the fishes by hanging them on different lengths of string.

7. Add the serpents to a central trunk shape made out of boxes to create your own 'snake tree'.

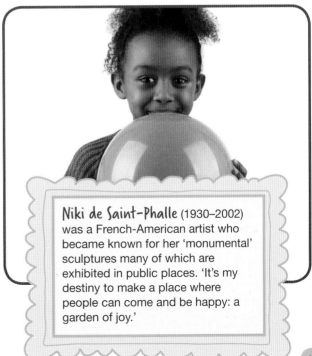

Niki de Saint-Phalle (1930–2002) was a French-American artist who became known for her 'monumental' sculptures many of which are exhibited in public places. 'It's my destiny to make a place where people can come and be happy: a garden of joy.'

Larger than life (Gormley)
Making model statues

What you need:

- Access online to images of 'Angel of the North', 'Another Place' by Gormley and his solo statues, e.g. 'Subject', 'Feel', 'Stand'
- Crêpe paper cut into long 'bandages'
- Garden wire
- Metal coat hangers
- Newspapers
- Cardboard tubes
- Camera

What to do:

1. Start by showing the children images of a variety of Gormley's sculptures. What do they all have in common? They are all human figures standing in space.

2. Let all the children find a space to stand and create their own statue pose. Will they stand up tall, point at something, hide their faces or place their hands on their hips and show some 'attitude'?

3. Ask for a volunteer child to stand still. Invite other children to mould them into a statue. Wrap them in crêpe paper bandages and take a photo of the 'living statue'.

4. Let the children work in groups using junk materials to create large-scale sculptures of human figures.

5. Show them how to use garden wire, metal coat hangers, rolls of newspaper, cardboard tubes and other junk. Be on call for joining parts together if needed.

6. Photograph the finished models, however they turn out!

Top tip ⭐

It helps to start with the head – use a circle bent out of a coat hanger or a balloon covered in papier-mâché.

What's in it for the children?

As they create statues with their bodies, children can show control, coordination and balance. Creating models will require different skills such as using tools and working together cooperatively.

Taking it forward

- Show children pictures of the 'WEEE Man' sculpture, housed at the Eden Project in Cornwall. It's a giant sculpture made out of waste electric and electronic equipment. Provide children with old CDs, circuit boards and other safe waste technology. Let them build recycled models using these materials.

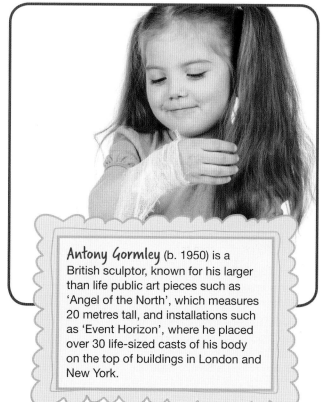

Antony Gormley (b. 1950) is a British sculptor, known for his larger than life public art pieces such as 'Angel of the North', which measures 20 metres tall, and installations such as 'Event Horizon', where he placed over 30 life-sized casts of his body on the top of buildings in London and New York.

Natural materials (Goldsworthy)

Now you see it, now you don't!

What you need:

- Access online to images of 'Balanced River Stones', 'Rowan Leaves and Hole', 'Broken Pebbles' by Goldsworthy
- An outside area, e.g. garden or park
- Scissors
- Camera

Top tip ★

Make sure you take plenty of pictures as well as allowing children to take some.

What's in it for the children?

They can work together as part of a group and talk about their ideas, choose different resources and show sensitivity to others' needs and feelings.

Taking it forward

- Look at the driftwood sculptures created by British artist James Doran Webb. Let children use lolly sticks, matchsticks, straws and found twigs to create their own sculptures. Use glue, tape, nails and wire to join materials together.

✚ Health & Safety

Remind children not to pick up any hazardous litter. Go on a separate litter pick with gloves and grabbers!

What to do:

1. Show the children some images of Goldsworthy's sculptures. Explain that they are not displayed in a gallery as they are 'temporary'. Once they are created, he photographs them and then moves on. Point out the shapes, sizes, patterns and colours he uses.

2. Go for a walk with the children in a garden or park. See what different natural materials they can find to use.

3. Challenge them to work in groups to create sculptures using leaves, stones or sticks.

4. Provide scissors so they can cut or trim materials. Can they create a shape, pattern, spiral or hole with the materials?

5. Let them arrange their chosen materials onto the ground and, when satisfied with the effect, take a photograph to record the finished work.

6. Take some materials back to your setting to continue the process.

7. Make a display using some of the children's ideas inside for others to appreciate.

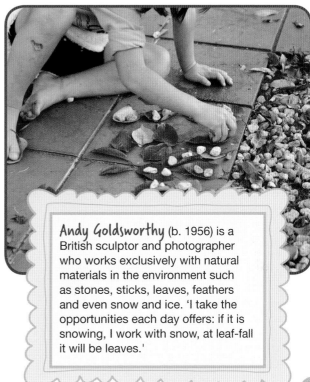

Andy Goldsworthy (b. 1956) is a British sculptor and photographer who works exclusively with natural materials in the environment such as stones, sticks, leaves, feathers and even snow and ice. 'I take the opportunities each day offers: if it is snowing, I work with snow, at leaf-fall it will be leaves.'

Flower 'mosaicks' (Delany)

Creating paper flowers

What you need:

- Access online to images of botanical collages of flowers by Delany
- Cut or dried flowers or plants
- Magnifying glasses
- Coloured chalks
- Black paper
- Coloured paper
- Scissors
- Tweezers
- Glue

What to do:

1. Show the children images of Delany's intricate 'mosaicks' of flowers. Explain that they are not paintings or pressed flowers but collages made using tiny pieces of paper.

2. Delany used to dissect the plants so she could see all the detail. Let the children handle and observe some real flowers close up using magnifying glasses. Identify and name the different parts.

3. Invite them to draw the rough outline of a flower or plant using chalks on black paper to start with.

4. Provide lots of different coloured paper for children to create their collages. Can they cut tiny petals out of one colour? Are all the petals exactly the same colour?

5. Let them use tweezers to pick up tiny pieces of paper to glue onto their collages.

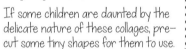

Top tip ★

If some children are daunted by the delicate nature of these collages, pre-cut some tiny shapes for them to use.

What's in it for the children?

Children can observe similarities and differences between flowers and plants and use control and coordination with a variety of tools to create their collages.

Taking it forward

- Try pressing some real flowers in a flower press, between kitchen paper sandwiched in a heavy book or even in the microwave! Let the children create some collages using these combined with pictures of flowers cut from seed catalogues.

- Look at the work of 'Flora Forager', Bridget Beth Collins, who uses flowers to create collages of different images such as birds and fish.

Mary Delany (1700–1788) created this technique – a precursor of collage – at the age of 72! She was a grieving widow who one day noticed that a piece of coloured paper exactly matched the fallen petal of a flower. 'I have invented a new way of imitating flowers.'

Painting with scissors (Matisse)

Cut out simple shapes

What you need:

- Leaves
- Minibeasts
- Magnifying glass or magnifying pot
- Access online to images of 'The Snail', 'Palmette' and 'La Gerbe' by Matisse
- Coloured paper
- Scissors

Top tip ⭐

Remind children that they can also use the bits of paper left after 'cutting out' as part of their artwork.

What's in it for the children?

Children can make observations of animals and plants and handle tools to create pictures and representations of what they see.

Taking it forward

- Watch a video on YouTube™ showing Matisse creating his cut-outs.
- Compare the cut-outs with the collage illustrations by Eric Carle in his children's books such as *The Very Hungry Caterpillar*.
- Read *Henri Matisse: Drawing with Scissors* by Jane O'Connor and find out more about the artist and his art.

✚ Health & Safety

Take care using scissors. Provide left-handed scissors where required.

What to do:

1. Go outside and find some big leaves. Look at some minibeasts using a magnifying glass or pot.
2. Show children a variety of Matisse's cut-out pictures online. Can they see the snail, the palm tree and the leaves in his cut-outs?
3. Talk about the shapes, colours, number of shapes, spiral layout, etc. involved in 'The Snail'.
4. Invite children to cut or tear coloured paper into squares and rectangles and create their own collage of a minibeast.
5. Use a large leaf to make a template and cut out one leaf in a very bright colour. Let children choose a contrasting background colour to mount the leaf on in the style of 'Palmette'.
6. Ask children to cut out lots of different-sized and different-coloured leaves using real leaves as templates.
7. Let children work in a group to create a large-scale collage using the cut-out leaves.
8. Spend time arranging the leaves in different ways before sticking them down.

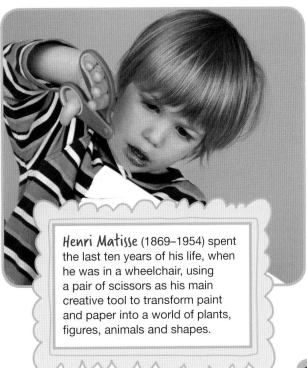

Henri Matisse (1869–1954) spent the last ten years of his life, when he was in a wheelchair, using a pair of scissors as his main creative tool to transform paint and paper into a world of plants, figures, animals and shapes.

Inside the box (Cornell)

Assembling treasures together in a box

What you need:

- Access online to images of 'The Hotel Eden' by Cornell
- Empty shallow boxes
- Selection of papers, e.g. newspaper, coloured paper, wallpaper, shiny paper, pages from old books, magazines, postcards, photographs, tickets
- Selection of small junk items, e.g. shells, pebbles, tiny toys, balls, corks, lids, driftwood, cotton reels, pompoms, dried flowers
- Glue, tape and string
- Bird templates
- Cardboard

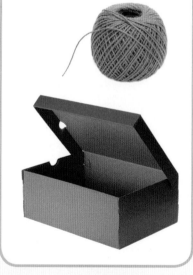

What to do:

1. Show the children images of Cornell's collage boxes, known as 'assemblage' art.

2. Talk about what materials they can see the artist has used – found objects, pictures, etc.

3. Let the children choose a shallow box or lid to use for their artwork. Select a variety of different types of paper to stick inside the box as a background.

4. Invite the children to choose a selection of items and arrange them in the box. Encourage the children to rearrange the objects several times until they are happy with their design.

5. Stick the chosen items into the box using glue, tape or string.

6. Choose a colourful bird picture and colour it in using bright colours.

7. Mount the bird on cardboard and hang it in the foreground of the box.

Top tip ⭐

Make sure the children are happy with the contents and arrangement of items in the box before they start fixing them!

What's in it for the children?

This activity is good for helping children to make individual choices about materials, layout and overall effect of their artwork. Some may prefer to work with a partner and collaborate together.

Taking it forward

- Make up a story to accompany the box. Ask children to connect some of the things in their box to create a narrative. Film the children telling each other their 'story box'.

- Look at the work of artist Kurt Schwitters, e.g. 'Opened by Customs', 'Pine Trees' or 'Untitled (Quality Street)'. He used papers and different found objects in his work. Let children create some more collages using these as inspiration.

✚ Health & Safety

Take care using scissors. Provide left-handed scissors where required.

Joseph Cornell (1903–1972) was a self-taught American artist and sculptor who is well-known for creating boxes or 'assemblage'. He spent most of his life in New York caring for his disabled brother. When he became famous, he held an exhibition of his work for children and served cakes and soft drinks at the opening!

Musical collage (Picasso)

Use shapes of musical instruments as inspiration

What you need:

- Access online to images of 'Guitar', 'Violin Hanging on the Wall' and 'Musical Score and Guitar' by Picasso
- Musical instruments, e.g. guitar, violin, ukulele, recorder and xylophone
- Paper and pencils
- Collage materials, e.g. cardboard, newspaper, manuscript paper, sheet music, wallpaper, string
- Scissors
- Glue

What to do:

1. Show children images of Picasso's various collages of guitars and other musical instruments.
2. Let children observe and handle the musical instruments.
3. Look at the shapes of the different instruments. Ask children to sketch some of their favourites with paper and pencils.
4. Make some templates of shapes for children to use and provide the art materials for children to select.
5. Let them choose the materials they want to use, cut different shapes and assemble their collage pictures before sticking them down.
6. Display their collages alongside the real instruments.

Top tip

Help cut out any tricky shapes from cardboard using a utility knife.

What's in it for the children?

They can observe, handle and listen to musical instruments before using mixed media and materials to create their own ideas.

Taking it forward

- Look at some of Georges Braque's collages that also featured musical instruments, e.g. 'Violin and Pipe' or 'La Mandolina'.
- Listen to some different musical instruments with the children.
- Picasso also used cardboard tubes, boxes, wire and string to construct or sculpt a 'silent guitar'. Provide lots of junk materials for the children to make a cardboard guitar. Can it make a sound? Try adding some elastic bands!

Pablo Picasso (1881–1973) was one of the first artists, along with his friend Georges Braque, to use the term 'collage', from the French word 'coller' – to glue or stick. They started by adding sand to their paint to change the texture and then stuck different papers on as well. 'Everything you can imagine is real.'

Photomontage (Höch)

Cut and paste photos and make a new face

What you need:

- Access online to images of 'Merry Woman', 'English Dancer' or 'Fashion Show' by Höch
- Old magazines, newspapers and photographs
- Scissors
- Glue

What's in it for the children?

Children will enjoy creating new faces and pictures by choosing different images and materials and presenting them in original ways.

Taking it forward

- Go to https://www.bbc.co.uk/cbbc/games/cbbc-picture-maker and let children use pictures, stickers and pens to create online pictures.

- Show children 'Walk on the Beach' by Sarah Eisenlohr and enjoy the way this artist plays with size. Let children bring in a photo of themselves from home, cut it out and add it to a background to create their own 'Walk on....' picture.

- Check out the work of John Stezaker who also cuts up photos to create new ones.

- Look at the works of Romare Bearden who used photomontage in his collages, e.g. 'Musicians' and 'Serenade'.

✚ Health & Safety

Take care using cutting tools. Provide left-handed scissors where required.

What to do:

1. Look at some examples of Höch's collages created by cutting up photographs in a style called photomontage. Do the children think they are funny?

2. Explain that Höch was one of the first artists to cut and paste photos to create new visions – a bit like 'photoshopping' today.

3. Provide photographs in magazines and newspapers showing lots of faces and figures.

4. Ask children to create their own 'mash-ups' of faces by cutting out features and sticking them together.

5. Try with some celebrity portraits. Can children still recognise the person?

6. Höch often had fun enlarging one particular feature in her pictures. Show children one of her most striking pictures: 'Bouquet of Eyes'.

7. Let the children choose and make a collage using lots of pictures of eyes, noses, ears or mouths.

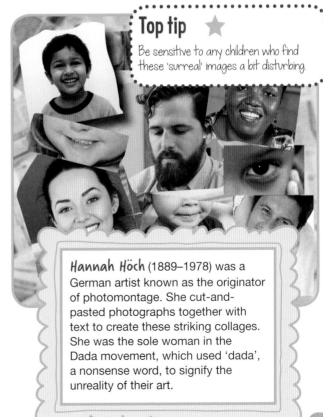

Top tip ★

Be sensitive to any children who find these 'surreal' images a bit disturbing.

Hannah Höch (1889–1978) was a German artist known as the originator of photomontage. She cut-and-pasted photographs together with text to create these striking collages. She was the sole woman in the Dada movement, which used 'dada', a nonsense word, to signify the unreality of their art.

Fallen paintings (Apfelbaum)
Create some large floor mosaics

What you need:

- Access online to images of 'Blossom', 'Blow Up', 'E' or 'Wonderbread' by Apfelbaum

- Large floor space

- Chalk

- Sweet wrappers

- Coloured cellophane

- Aluminium foil

- Scissors

- Variety of materials such as crushed velvet, cotton and silk

- Fabric paints or dye

- Camera

Top tip

Try to find a space to use that won't need to be cleared up at the end of the day, as this activity should be revisited over a few days!

What's in it for the children?

Children can work together in a large group to create a temporary artwork, demonstrating good cooperative skills.

Taking it forward

- Look at images of traditional patchwork, joining strips, squares and other shaped pieces together usually into quilts or pictures.

- Try some other mosaic art using tiny pieces of coloured paper or glass glued onto a tile base.

✚ Health & Safety

Take care using cutting tools. Provide left-handed scissors where required.

What to do:

1. Show children images of some 'Fallen paintings' or giant floor mosaics made by Apfelbaum. Talk about what they can see. What is unusual about these artworks? What materials do they think she has used?

2. Choose a shape with the children and draw a large outline on the floor in chalk. Alternatively, start from the centre and let the shape evolve as they work.

3. Choose a type of material. Start with sweet wrappers, cellophane and aluminium foil. Let children take turns to lay the pieces down, trying to overlap them so there are no gaps. Don't use glue – just let the pieces lie on the floor.

4. Take photos as you go along to record the different shapes and pictures created.

5. Try some fabric mosaics. Cut strips of material: cotton, velvet or silk. Sort into piles of similar colours.

6. Experiment with fabric paints and dyes to create different shades of colour.

7. Let children take turns to place materials down onto the floor to create a mosaic shape out of the patchwork strips.

Polly Apfelbaum (b. 1955) is an American contemporary artist who specialises in large scale installations consisting of lots of hand-cut pieces of crushed velvet arranged on the floor. She calls these 'Fallen paintings' – a sort of merger between painting and sculpture.

Kaleidoscopic collage (Milhazes)

Using layers of paper and packaging

What you need:

- Access online to images of 'Liberty', 'Yogurt', 'Fruit' or 'Manjary' by Milhazes
- Paper and card
- Wrapping paper
- Sweet wrappers
- Packaging
- Circle and flower templates
- Scissors
- String
- CDs
- Silk flowers
- Christmas baubles

Top tip ★

Encourage children to bring in favourite sweet wrappers or packing from home to use.

What's in it for the children?

Children will explore different media and materials in original ways to create collages. They can also select and use technology to create art.

Taking it forward

- Provide some real kaleidoscopes for children to handle and look through. Can they describe what they can see to a partner or the group?
- Go to https://permadi.com/java/spaint/spaint.html and encourage children to try some online kaleidoscope art.

What to do:

1. Show the children images of the colourful mixed-media collages by Milhazes. What materials can they see in 'Fruit' or 'Manjary'?

2. Explain that they are going to work together to create a 'kaleidoscope' collage.

3. Provide children with a selection of materials – wrapping paper, shiny card, coloured paper and sweet wrappers. Use these to create a stripy block background on a piece of card.

4. Show them how to use circle and flower templates to cut out shapes to layer on the top.

5. Help children to create some more swirly shapes such as leaves, spirals and rings. Cut some out of shiny paper and add another layer to the collage.

6. Look at Milhazes's mobile 'Gamboa'. Work together to create a hanging curtain or mobile by attaching circles of different sizes and materials onto lengths of string.

7. Add old CDs, silk flowers and Christmas baubles to create more variety and texture.

Beatriz Milhazes (b. 1960) is a Brazilian artist who creates vibrant mixed-media collages inspired by Brazilian folk art.

Souper printing (Warhol)

Combining collage and printing

What you need:

- Access online to 'Campbell's Soup Cans', 'Marilyn Diptych' and 'Flowers' by Warhol
- Large paper
- Paints and brushes
- Shallow trays
- Polystyrene tiles
- Flower templates
- Coloured paper
- Food labels from tins and bottles
- Scissors

What to do:

1. Show children images of Warhol's pictures and explain how he used screen-printing to create the repeated images.

2. Try some of these activities with the children to create repeated images.

3. Start by making a repeated handprint picture. Divide a large piece of paper into eight equal sections.

4. Ask children to paint each section or box a different colour.

5. Then add a handprint in a contrasting colour inside each box.

6. Try creating a tile to print a repeated pattern by drawing a picture onto a polystyrene tile using a pencil.

7. Make repeated press prints of the tile in different colours.

8. Use flower templates and coloured paper to create a repeated collage of flower shapes.

9. Create a repeated collage using labels from food tins and bottles.

Top tip ★

Don't forget that when using press print tiles, the images will appear in reverse.

What's in it for the children?

Children will use a variety of materials and methods to produce repeated images in artwork that they can count, collate and compare.

Taking it forward

- Create a display using all the different repeated images the children have produced.

- Look at 'Cow Wallpaper' designed by Warhol. Let children try creating their own wallpaper design on strips of lining paper using repeated printing patterns. Let them use prints and inkpads, potato prints, shape cutters or other simple press prints.

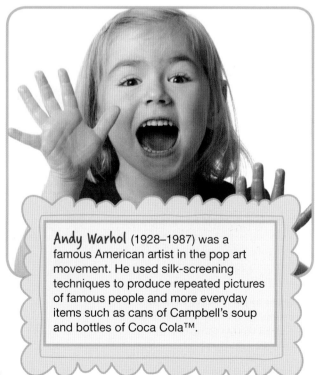

Andy Warhol (1928–1987) was a famous American artist in the pop art movement. He used silk-screening techniques to produce repeated pictures of famous people and more everyday items such as cans of Campbell's soup and bottles of Coca Cola™.

Cartoon art (Lichtenstein)

Use comic book graphics to create word posters

What you need:

- Access online to images of 'Whaam!' and 'Explosion' by Lichtenstein
- Comics
- Paper
- Felt pens
- Computers or tablets

Top tip ★

Children can use all capital letters for their word to add emphasis, or a mixture of lower and upper case.

What's in it for the children?

Children can explore the sounds of words and use ICT to create a contemporary style of artwork.

Taking it forward

- Show children a copy of Lichtenstein's 'Hot Dog'. It looks like a sign for a fast food shop. Patrick Caulfield was another artist who painted 'popular' things in a pop art style. Look at his painting 'Sweet Bowl'. Ask children to choose a favourite food to draw or paint using bold and bright colours.

What to do:

1. Look at some of Lichtenstein's paintings and artworks. They often use very simple shapes, cartoons or words as part of the image.

2. Compare this with how words are displayed in children's comics using graphics to emphasise their sound such as POP, WHAM or BANG!

3. Make a collection of sound words with the children.

4. Ask children to choose a sound word, write it out in the middle of the page and then use layers of strong coloured outlines to make the word appear louder!

5. Repeat the activity using their name as the central word on the poster.

6. Let children use ICT to produce art using different fonts, colours and typography. How many different ways can they write one word?

7. Display the word posters around the room.

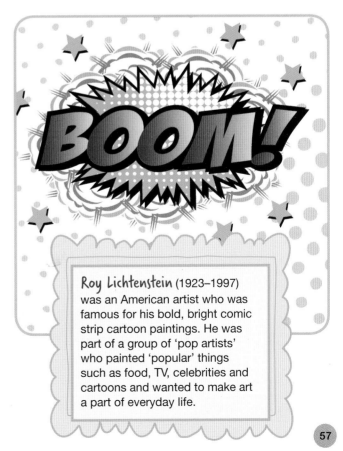

Roy Lichtenstein (1923–1997) was an American artist who was famous for his bold, bright comic strip cartoon paintings. He was part of a group of 'pop artists' who painted 'popular' things such as food, TV, celebrities and cartoons and wanted to make art a part of everyday life.

Dancing dogs *(Haring)*
Simple chalk graffiti drawings

What you need:

- Access online to images of Haring's stylised pictures of people, cats and dogs
- White chalks
- Blackboards or paper
- Coloured chalks
- Wall space
- Cardboard
- Paint and brushes
- Black felt pens

What to do:

1. Look at images online of Haring's most famous pictures including 'Dancing dogs' and 'Radiant Baby'.

2. Explain that Haring started off by drawing in white chalk on blackboards or empty walls.

3. Let children try drawing, writing and creating pictures with white chalk on blackboards or black paper. Can they create their own special signature or 'tag'?

4. Go outside and let them draw and write using coloured chalk on walls or pavements.

5. They can draw emojis, cartoon faces, stick people and animals. Write a word and then enlarge it using layers of colour – see Cartoon art p.57.

6. Make cardboard templates of Haring's dog and men for children to draw around and paint.

7. They can choose bold colours to paint the figures and then go over the outline in black felt pen.

8. Point out how the artist adds extra black lines to create the idea of movement. Help children to use this technique to improve their artwork.

Top tip ⭐

Make sure you talk about when it is okay to draw on walls and when it is not!

✚ Health & Safety

Take care that the images you select to share with the children are suitable as some of Haring's work has an adult theme.

What's in it for the children?

Creating pictures and writing on walls and pavements will help children to make progress with their literacy skills alongside their artistic development.

Taking it forward

- Go to http://www.haringkids.com/coloringbook/index.html and let children create their own Haring-style pictures online to colour or print.

- Use a tablet to go to https://www.tate.org.uk/kids/games-quizzes/street-art and help children to create their own street art at the Tate using virtual stickers, stamps, spray cans and rollers.

- Look at and compare work by other famous street artists such as Banksy, Tyrone Wright ('Rone') or Edgar Müller. Choose three striking pieces and let children choose a favourite.

Keith Haring (1958–1990) was an American artist who started drawing in New York subways and his quirky cartoon style pictures of babies, flying saucers and 'dancing dogs' soon captured people's imagination.

Lollipop trees (Hundertwasser)

Making maps and models

What you need:

- Access online to images of 'A Crossroads', 'Blobs grow in Beloved Gardens' and 'Kreative Architektur' by Hundertwasser
- Coloured chalks
- Black paper
- Magazines
- Cardboard boxes
- Paint
- Glue
- Dowels/old pencils
- Wool

Top tip

Don't let the weather stop the art. Using chalk outside on a wet day makes the colours shine even more brightly.

What's in it for the children?

Children can observe their environment, see similarities and differences, and use their imaginations to express what they see.

Taking it forward

- Look at images of the Hundertwasser House in Vienna. Would the children like to live in a house like this? What do they imagine it would be like inside?

- Look at some other paintings of trees such as 'Tree of Life' by Klimt, 'The Red Tree' by Mondrian and 'Olive Trees' by Van Gogh.

What to do:

1. Show children an image of Hundertwasser's painting 'A Crossroads'. Talk about what they can see in the picture.

2. Go outside and draw a crossroads on the playground. Arrange sit-and-ride toys in the junctions and create a living 'crossroads'.

3. Use chalks, black paper and pictures of vehicles to create collage versions of the crossroads.

4. Hundertwasser used spirals in all his work. Encourage children to go outside and draw multi-coloured spirals on the ground using chalks. How many different colours can they include in their spiral?

5. Paint spirals on black paper using lots of different colours.

6. Look at 'Blobs Grow in Beloved Gardens'. Let children make their own lollipop trees using cardboard and brightly coloured paints.

7. Cut two cardboard circles and glue them together with a piece of dowelling or old pencil as a trunk.

8. Paint spirals onto the circles or blobs. Squirt spirals of glue on top and stick on coloured spirals of wool.

Friedensreich Hundertwasser (1928–2000) was an Austrian artist, painter and architect. His paintings use vibrant colours and wacky forms and the 'lollipop trees' and 'onion domes' are especially appealing to children. 'I fill a picture until it is full with magic!'

iPad® art (Hockney)

Finger painting on a tablet

What you need:

- Access online to images of some of Hockney's iPad® art including landscapes and still life
- iPads® or tablets
- Art apps, e.g. Drawing Pad or SketchBook

Top tip ⭐

Check that the app you are using has an automatic save option so children don't lose their valuable artwork.

What's in it for the children?

Children will use technology to create artworks and express their ideas about what they can see around them.

Taking it forward

- Show children 'Pearblossom Highway', a collage picture created by Hockney out of over 700 small photographs! Let the children experiment with the camera. Help them to take a series of pictures that can be stuck together to create one image.

- Look at other paintings by Hockney created before he started using the iPad®, such as 'Nichols Canyon', a colourful landscape painting of a scene in the Hollywood Hills in California and 'A Bigger Splash', part of series of paintings of swimming pools.

What to do:

1. Look at images of Hockney's iPad® art and watch him drawing on the iPad® on YouTube™.

2. Let children use any available art apps for the tablet to produce their own artwork.

3. Encourage them to experiment using finger painting, drawing using different tools such as coloured pencils, brushes and rollers and adding stickers.

4. Try some other art apps such as Kapu Bloom Tunes, which combines finger painting with music, or Toontastic, which allows children to make their own animated cartoons on the screen.

5. Use an interactive whiteboard to share the children's artwork with the whole group.

6. Print off a selected piece for each child to show in an exhibition of iPad® art.

David Hockney (b. 1937) is an English artist, painter and photographer. He started creating art on the iPad® in 2010 using the Brushes app and these pictures have been shown in several exhibitions around the world.

Yarn bombing (Sayeg)

Using wool and string to make pictures

What you need:

- Access online to Sayeg's website: http://www. magdasayeg.com
- Yarn
- String
- Ribbons
- Strips of fabric
- Coloured paper
- Pieces of cardboard
- Scissors
- Twigs

What to do:

1. Show children examples of work by the textile artist Sayeg. She is known as the mother of 'yarn bombing' – using yarn or wool to cover items either for decoration or as a type of art installation.

2. Provide children with lots of yarn and other textile materials and let them create textile collages.

3. Try some weaving. Create a loom from pieces of cardboard packaging with slits cut into opposite ends. Help children to tie pieces of wool across the length of the card.

4. Show them how to weave yarn, string, ribbon, strips of fabric, and coloured paper in and out of the wool on the loom.

5. Go outside and look for twigs which branch and create V or Y shapes.

6. Show children how to tie wool onto the twigs and weave in-between the branches.

7. Take some twigs inside and let children use lots of different coloured yarn to create their own yarn bombing inside and outside.

Top tip ⭐

Let the children have lots of practice tying simple knots before they try to make the looms independently.

✚ Health & Safety

Take care using sharp tools for cutting and/or sewing.

What's in it for the children?

Children will develop good control and coordination in small movements as they create their woven artworks.

Taking it forward

- Look at 'Disenchanted Forest' by Angela Bulloch. Explain to the children that you are going to create your own string forest or maze. Find a corner in the room with lots of points where you can attach string or balls of yarn. Help children to weave strands of coloured yarn up and down and through each other. Alternatively, use a hula hoop and create a yarn spider web.

- Try some other textile collage using Binca fabric, embroidery threads, buttons, beads, and so on. Show children how to sew in and out of the holes in the fabric and attach beads and buttons as they go.

- Look at the work of Benjamin Shine, a British artist who 'paints' with fabric at https://www.benjaminshine.com/projects_to_view/tulle-sacred-giant.html.

Magda Sayeg, the American artist who started 'guerrilla knitting' or 'yarn bombing' movement in 2004, began knitting in her teens. She creates temporary and permanent installations covering buildings, works of art and even buses with yarn!

Shapes and shadows (Parker)

Shining a light onto shifting shapes

What you need:

- Access online to images of 'Cold Dark Matter', 'The Brass Band' and 'Thirty Pieces of Silver' by Parker

- Chalk

- Lamps and torches

- Black paper

- Scissors

- Selection of metal utensils, e.g. forks, spoons, plates, sieves, whisks

- String

- Garden wire

- Wire frame, hat stand or clothes rail

Top tip ⭐

Ask children to bring in metal utensils and pots from home that you can use to create an installation.

What's in it for the children?

They will explore features of their environment and observe changes in relation to places, objects and materials. They can safely experiment with design, texture, form and function.

Taking it forward

- Extend the children's experience of their hanging artwork by exploring its use as a musical instrument. Let children tap and shake the different suspended items. Add some wooden objects to create a visual and sound contrast. Record the sounds they create.

What to do:

1. Look at some of Parker's installations online. Explain that to create 'Cold Dark Matter' she arranged for a garden shed to be blown up and then suspended all the pieces in the air around a light bulb and used the lighting to create shadows.

2. How do the children think that the artist made 'The Brass Band' or 'Thirty Pieces of Silver'? (The metal items were flattened by steamroller before being suspended on wires.)

3. Go outside on a sunny day and explore shadows. Point out shadows made by buildings, play equipment or plants.

4. Let children observe and draw around their own shadows using chalk.

5. Set up a lamp inside or use a torch and let children create shadows on the wall using their hands or shapes cut out of black paper.

6. Work together to select metal utensils and attach them to different lengths of string or wire.

7. Suspend the different metal objects from a wire frame, hat stand or empty clothes rail.

8. Display the installation in a room with lamps shining on it to create shadows on the wall.

Cornelia Parker (b. 1956) is an award-winning English sculptor and artist, famous for creating large-scale installations full of variety and imagination.